An Episcopal Odyssey

Arnold Harris Mathew

Republished by the Saint Gabriel Theological Press
In cooperation with Lulu Enterprises, Inc.
2010

ISBN: 978-0-557-49267-1

Forward from the Publisher

This is a re-print of the original work by Archbishop Arnold Harris Mathew. It is presented in the original form through transcription, and any errors are as in the first edition.

It is the publisher's hope that this work can be some small contribution to the Old Catholic Movement. It is essential for the proper study and evaluation of the Movement to have ready access to primary sources. This work, in Archbishop Mathew's own words, details his personal story and reasoning for taking certain actions.

Although Archbishop Mathew has been viewed as both saint and villain in his own lifetime and afterwards, his conviction is very evident in this work. This publication is dedicated to him.

Adésto supplicatiónibus nostris, omnópotens Deus:
ut, quod humilitatis nostræ geréndum est ministério,
tuæ virtútis impleátur efféctu.
Per Dóminum nostrum Jesum Christum, Filium tuum :
qui tecum vivit et regnat in unitáte Spíritus Sancti Deus,
per ómnia sæcula sæculórum.

- From the Mass for the Consecration of a Bishop

William Myers
May 28, 2010

Ergo inimicus vobis factus sum verum dicens vobis.

"AN EPISCOPAL ODYSSEY."

AN OPEN LETTER
TO
HIS GRACE
THE RIGHT HON. AND MOST REV.
RANDALL THOMAS DAVIDSON, D.D.,
LORD ARCHBISHOP OF CANTERBURY,
PRIMATE OF THE CHURCH OF ENGLAND AND
METROPOLITAN, ETC., ETC., ETC.

BY
ARNOLD HARRIS MATHEW
ARCHBISHOP OF THE OLD ROMAN CATHOLIC RITE
IN GREAT BRITAIN AND IRELAND
DE JURE 4TH EARL OF LANDAFF OF THOMASTOWN, CO.
TIPPERARY

PRICE FOURPENCE

TO BE OBTAINED FROM THE SECRETARY,
THE BRAMBLES, KINGSDOWN

MY LORD ARCHBISHOP,

I have already informed Your Grace that it would be necessary for me to address to you "an open letter." The necessity has been occasioned by your publication in the *Guardian* of 19th August, 1915, of a letter which you caused your Chaplain to address to me last May, together with a "memorandum" by which that letter was accompanied.

In order that it may be possible to form an opinion on the ingenious implications of the article in question, and incidentally of the good taste displayed in these documents, and in their publication in the press, I reproduce them *in extenso* :--

AN EPISCOPAL ODYSSEY.

The Archbishop of Canterbury and Bishop Mathew.

As misunderstanding appears to exist in America, and possible in England, regarding the history and status of Right Rev. A. H. Mathew, who was consecrated in 1908 by Old Catholic Bishops in Holland with a view to some form of Episcopal ministry in England, the Archbishop of Canterbury has transmitted to the Presiding Bishop of the Protestant Episcopal Church in the United States a copy of the appended letter and Memorandum recently sent by the Archbishop's direction to Bishop Mathew:--

"Lambeth Palace, S.E., May 11th, 1915.

"Right Reverend and Dear Sir,---I am directed by the Archbishop of Canterbury to send to you, in accordance with an intimation already given to you by the Bishop of London, a reply to certain recent letters which you have addressed to his Grace and the Bishop of London. If the Archbishop understands the purport of these letters aright, their suggestion is that you and those who are present associated with you should be regarded as constituting or representing the Holy Catholic Church in this country, the Church of England remaining as a religious body associated with the national life, but with no claim to a regular or orthodox position in any ecclesiastical sense. You further suggest that the Bishop of London should submit himself to you for re-Ordination, in which case you would be prepared, as the Archbishop understands, to grant him some official recognition. The Archbishop of Canterbury feels it to be hardly possible to treat these letters seriously or to reply to them otherwise than in terms which you would regard as more discourteous than the silence which you depreciate. But as you press for a reply, the Archbishop thinks it best that I should, on his behalf, enclose to you a memorandum recalling in bare outline some of the incidents of the last eight years. In view of the facts which are therein referred to, the Archbishop feels it to be impossible for him to enter with you into a discussion of the subjects raised, or to regard your letters on these public matters as bearing a confidential character. He is quite willing, therefore, that you should make this letter and the memorandum public if you desire to do so, and he reserves to himself a similar discretion.—I have the honor to be, Right Reverend and Dear Sir, your obedient Servant,

"J. V. MACMILLAN, Chaplain.

"The Right Reverend Bishop Mathew."

Roman Priest and Anglican Curate.

The following is the Memorandum referred to:--The Archbishop of Canterbury first heard from the Rev. A. H. Mathew in July, 1907, when Mr. Mathew, who was then fifty-four years of age and described himself as *de jure* Earl of Landaff, asked whether he could be given some ministerial charge in the Church of England, the Church of his Baptism and boyhood. He recounted his preparation in youth for the Anglican ministry, his Ordination to the priesthood in the Church of Rome (1877), his marriage in 1892, his re-admission to the Church of England, and his temporary service, under the name it would seem of Count Povoleri, in a London curacy with the sanction of Bishop Temple. He had subsequently, he said, lived quietly in the country, discarding clerical dress and doing no ministerial work. He desired to assure the Archbishop that he repudiated Papal claims, that he entertained no doubt about Anglican Orders, and that his wish would be to hold an Incumbency in the Church of England. When the Archbishop explained that, in addition to adequate testimony to personal character, about which there would obviously be no difficulty, there must be some period of probationary and subordinate work before the question of such nomination as had been suggested could be even considered, Mr. Mathew replied, not unnaturally, that he preferred to abandon the project and to remain in the position in which he then was. The Archbishop accepted the conclusion, assuring Mr. Mathew that he was not precluded from re-opening the question at a future date should he so desire. Mr. Mathew took occasion to reiterate his conviction about the Church of Rome:--"The Papacy," he wrote (August 12, 1907) "instead of being the 'visible centre of unity,' I regard as the centre and origin of ecclesiastical discord and disunion, the fomenter of schisms, and the seat of ecclesiastical despotism and tyranny."

Old Catholic Bishop.

A few months later (December 30, 1907) he wrote:--"I have definitely decided to throw in my lot with the Old Catholics. We shall open a Mission in this country for the benefit of those Roman Catholics who are unable to continue conscientious adhesion to the Vatican, and this we shall do in a spirit of perfect and cordial amity for the Church of England and in no spirit of aggression, still les proselytism…I am now in correspondence with the Archbishop of Utrecht, who will formally authorize the formation of a ranch of the Church in Great Britain on the lines I have indicated." In this reply the Archbishop wrote:-- " I do not gather that there is any step which you now desire me to take in the matter. I am, of course, at all times glad to learn of any movement within the Church of Rome in the direction of sounder principles of doctrine and usage. But, believing as I do that the Church of England is in this country the true representative of the Catholic Church as it comes down to us from the past, I can hardly be expected to look favorably upon the establishment in England of another Society claiming that position, even though it does so in a less exclusive and arrogant spirit than that which finds its centre and expression in the

Vatican." Other letters followed, but no intimation was given of any proposed Episcopal Consecration until, on April 8th, 1908, the Archbishop received, presumably from Mr. Mathew, a lithographed card stating that on that very day his "Episcopal Consecration" would take place at Utrecht. It did not at once take place, for the reason, as was stated on behalf of the Old Catholic Bishops, that they had unexpectedly become aware of the fact that Mr. Mathew was a married man. The Consecration, however, took place at Utrecht on April 28, 1908.

From Old Catholic Bishop to French Archbishop.

It has seemed to be right that those first incidents should be recorded in some detail, but the subsequent story does not appear to be of sufficient importance to make it necessary to narrate its particulars. It is not evident that any public purpose would be served by an endeavour to explain the successive changes of designation which preceded and followed the breach which very speedily took place between Bishop Mathew and the Old Catholic Bishops, and that between Bishop Mathew and (it would appear) most of those who would for a time claimed to have received presbyterial or Episcopal Orders at his hands. The Archbishop of Canterbury has been, and still is, the recipient of applications from one after another of these. They contend that they had acted under a misapprehension, and that they hope that the Archbishop of Canterbury may be able to in some way to relieve them, a request with which it is not easy to comply. Writing to the

Archbishop in May, 1909, Bishop Mathew claimed to be simply an Old Catholic Bishop. "I neither desired nor sought," he writes, "Episcopal Consecration. I was completely deceived and entirely mislead by -----, a man who has deceived many besides myself.... Although I was certainly consecrated under misapprehension, I have been anxious that my office should not in any way be abused." After his complete breach with the Old Catholics of Holland in 1910, he describes himself as "Catholic Bishop" or, again, as "Bishop in England and Ireland of the English Catholic Church," called a few weeks later "The Western Orthodox Catholic Church in Great Britain and Ireland." Shortly afterwards the title used is "Archbishop of London." In March, 1911, the title is "Archbishop and Metropolitan of the English Catholic Church." This became "The Catholic Church in England, Latin Uniate Branch," and, two months later, "The Catholic Church in England Latin and Orthodox United," under a leader described as "Archbishop of England," and subsequently as "Sa Grandeur Mgr. A. H. Mathieu, Archevêque de Londres, Comte de Landave, Metropolitain de Grand-Bretagne et d'Irlande, Evêque provisoire de l'Eglise Catholique Française."

A Handsome Offer.

Accounts of Bishop Mathew's relation to the Roman Catholic Church were given in documents produced in the course of the unsuccessful libel action brought by Bishop Mathew against the *Times* newspaper in 1913, the grounds of action being the publication by the *Times* of the following words used in a Papal document connected with the excommunication of two priests who had claimed to have received Episcopal Consecration from Bishop Mathew:--"Nor was this information left without authentic testimony, for the person who was the chief author of this sacrilegious misdeed—a certain pseudo-Bishop named Arnold Harris Mathew—was not ashamed to confirm the fact in letters, full of self-assumption, which he has addressed to us. This person has, moreover, thought fit to bestow upon himself the title of Anglo-Catholic Archbishop of London." The present attitude and policy of Bishop Mathew is perhaps sufficiently indicated by the following quotation from one of his published utterances during the present year:--"The Catholic party in the Established religion of Queen Elizabeth will be invited to come into union with us.... For this work we received our Mission from the spiritual descendants of the British Apostle of the Netherlands, St. Willibrord. We are both willing and hopeful that this work may be carried out in union with the Holy See. If his Holiness Pope Benedict XV., who is a Pontiff of high times, will deign to listen to us, and to assist us with his approval, his Holiness will have no reason to regret the confidence he may repose in us... In no other way can the British Empire be restored to Catholic unity." It is presumably in connection with this scheme that Bishop Mathew now invites the Bishop of London to submit himself to him for re-Ordination, and expresses to the Archbishop of Canterbury his readiness to act with amity towards the Bishops of the Church of England, provided that

Bishop Mathew and those at present associated with him be recognized as the representatives of the Holy Catholic Church in this country.

May 11, 1915 J. V. M.

There are two things I wish to say about my letters to Your Grace and to the Bishop of London, referred to in the above article.

1.—They were marked "PRIVATE," and written in confidence and in the belief that they would meet with gentleman like treatment at your Lordship's hands.

2.—They were written in the hope of bringing about an amicable understanding, whereby we might co-operate with you in good works, and perhaps set forward in some small degree the great work of Reunion.

I, my Lord Archbishop, have reached the eventide of life, when the shadows begin to gather round, the world's illusions, vanities and wickedness become more fully realized, and the end of warfare and strife draws nearer.

Neither you nor the Bishop of London thought it worthwhile to take the slightest notice of my appeal to your Lordships, beyond rendering assistance to my persecutors and publishing the above discourteous biographical sketch.

One cannot refrain from expressing the intense surprise and sorrow one feels that, at a time of National crisis like the present, when our beloved Country is pouring out her life's blood in a desperate struggle for existence, and for the protection of all that is good, and that makes life worth living, the Primate of the Established Church can find time to trifle with one's family affairs and the "history" of one's career.

It is only less astonishing than the favour shown and the credence given to a certain disreputable curate, whom I regret to mention because he is dead. He was the great enemy of our work, and your Grace's chief informant against us.

I shall occasion to refer to this unfortunate man again in this letter, when it will, alas, be necessary to say something of his private life.

So far, I have suffered in silence, knowing that my defense must necessarily reveal something of the sins and vices of certain men, who have constituted themselves our enemies, and so have caused grave scandal and injury to Religion.

However, I feel that the time has arrive when I ought to yield to the entreaties of my faithful friends, and answer, once and for all, the charges continually brought against me by your Grace and by certain others in co-operation with you.

I will, therefore, proceed to explain my actions and give the reasons for the various "charges" I am accused of making,* in the order in which they are cited in your letter and "memorandum." In so doing I am confident that, in every case, my explanation will

---

* Your Grace was born of Presbyterian parents in Edinburgh. You received the Presbyterian rite of "baptism" when a month old, and you remained a member of the Kirk until, as a young man, you decided to change your religion, which you did by attending the services of the Church of England, and then entering its ministry.

refute the insinuations with which your article abounds.

The document opens by stating that "misunderstanding appears to exist in America and possibly in England" as to my history and status!

What are the facts? They are as follows:--

A few of my Clergy have visited America—one or two of them have remained there. In January last one of my auxiliaries, the Prince de Landas, after an examination of his credentials, was invited by an American Protestant Episcopalian Bishop to take part in the consecration of a Protestant Episcopalian Missionary Bishop, in New York.

He did so without my knowledge or sanction. It would see that the American Church was disposed to give us a fair hearing,--a piece of justice of which, thanks to our enemies, we have had very little experience at home.

In 1910 we found it necessary to sever our connection with the Continental Old Catholics and so declare our autonomy. Our reasons for doing will be given at length when I deal with the matter a little later on. The point is, that my speech, at the Congress held in Vienna in September, 1909, in which I maintained the necessity of repelling Protestant innovations, both in teaching and in practice together with my subsequent separation from the Protestantising Old Catholics in 1910, caused no little annoyance to the Continental Old Catholic Bishops, and, it would seem, to Bishop Herzog, the German Bishop at Berne, in particular.

No sooner do our enemies perceive that the American Episcopal Church is willing to extend to us that friendly hospitality which is an integral part of the American character, than they at once contrive to throw dust in the eyes of our American Friends.

Under colour of giving first-hand information, calculated to clear up any "misunderstanding" about me, your Grace writes an article complained of, with the deliberate intention of persuading the American Church that I am a thoroughly unreliable and untrustworthy person. In short, you imply that I am a religious adventurer and outcast, who from time to time to time has been driven to make many "changes" for some questionable purpose.

Dr. Herzog, whom I annoyed by resisting his German Protestantism, and whose chief grievance against me seems to be that I am "an Englishman," united with you, or you with him, and states that my consecration was obtained "by fraud," and is consequently "null and void"!

It is perfectly true that certain statistical misrepresentations as to our numbers were made to the Old Catholic Bishops by a suspended priest, who has recently been excommunicated, but I was in no way privy to them. As soon after my consecration as I discovered this unhappy state of affairs, I immediately put the matter before my consecrator, and *offered to resign and retire once more into private life*, which I had reluctantly left owing to my election and consecration.

No better answer could be found to Dr. Herzog's newest charges than the following letter from the Continental Old Catholic Bishops—of whom, please observe, Dr. Herzog is one—which appeared in the English "Guardian," under date, June 3rd, 1908.

"AN OLD CATHOLIC BISHOP FOR ENGLAND.

SIR,

We, the Archbishop and Bishops of the Old Catholic Church of Holland, and the Old Catholic Bishops of Germany and Switzerland, having heard with much concern of certain events connected with our English branch of the Old Catholic Church, wish to say that we have been in correspondence with a suspended Roman Catholic priest in England since the year 1902.

This priest visited the Bishops of Bonn, Berne, Haarlem, Deventer, and the Archbishop of Utrecht, and we believed him to be in perfect accord with us. He accompanied Bishop Mathew on his visit to the Archbishop of Utrecht. On April 7th in the present year he, with others, signed the petition to the Bishops begging us to consecrate the Right Rev. A. H. Mathew.

All the documents were sent by this priest to Bishop Herzog, accompanied by numerous letters urging upon us the immediate need of a Bishop, not only for the requirements of his own congregation, but for those of other clergy and congregations specified by him. We had no reason to suppose that we were mistaken in complying with his request. We wish now to state that our confidence in Bishop Mathew remains unshaken, after carefully perusing a large number of the documents bearing upon this matter, and we earnestly hope that his ministrations will be abundantly blessed by Almighty God, and that he will receive the cordial support of the British people and Church in the trying circumstances in which he has been placed.

In the name of the Old Catholic Bishops of Holland, Germany, and Switzerland,*

The Secretary,
+ J. J. VAN THIEL,
Bishop of Haarlem."

---

* The following quotations are from an article on "England," which appeared on July 9th, 1910, in Der Katholik, the organ of the Swiss "Old Catholics," or as they prefer to be called, "Christian Catholics," over whom Dr. Herzog presides. They furnish yet another proof of Dr. Herzog's inconsistency, and of the futility of his latest argument against the validity of my consecration, for they clearly show that neither Dr. Herzog not his adherents had suggested any doubt as to my consecration at this time, i.e., two years after the publication of the above letter from all the Old Catholic Bishops, exonerating me from all blame as to the statistical misrepresentations made at my consecration:--"It is to be understood," says Der Katholik, " as a matter of course, that we must leave with Bishop Mathew the responsibility for what he says and does. We ourselves have not denied the validity of Anglican Orders, and we seek for our adherents among the Catholic members of our own confession.—Bishop Mathew's organization may be a welcome haven for many Roman Catholics in England, who, though dissatisfied with papal jurisdiction would be indisposed to subscribe to the 39 Articles."

No one has ever expressed any doubt as to the validity of my consecration, excepting Dr. Herzog and those amateur "theologians" who have recently (1915) been influenced by him. Even he did not put forward any "doubts" until after the outbreak of the great War, and that he does so now is doubtless due to the fact that the German Bishop at Berne is suffering from Anglophobia.

I may add that, had the slightest doubt existed amongst the Old Catholic Bishops, as to the validity of my consecration, they would certainly not have invited me, as they did, to assist as a co-consecrator, at the consecration of Mgr. John Kowalski, at Utrecht, in October, 1909, nor should I have been most cordially again requested to assist at the consecration of his two Suffragans, Mgr. Prochniewski and Mgr. Golembiowski, at Plotsk, in 1910, but in this instance I did not assist, the distance from England being too great.

So far, as I am able to judge, the only "misunderstanding" which can possibly exist, either in America or elsewhere, is that which has been invented by Your Grace, by Dr. Herzog and by certain others, who are our enemies, and any such "misunderstanding" has been suggested deliberately,--for your carefully constructed article is of no real help or value either to the American Church or to individuals seeking the truth about my personal history or concerning our movement. It simply intensifies difficulties, and fosters misunderstanding, and that it might do so appears to me to be the express purpose for which it was written.

Your Grace does *not* understand aright the purport of my letters to you and to the Bishop of London. We are not so absurd as to claim to be, exclusively, "THE Holy Catholic Church in this Country"!

What, then, do we claim to be?

We claim to be precisely what we are, viz.:--

A very humble little Catholic *Mission*, possessing indisputable Orders and valid Sacraments, working side by side with the great Roman Catholic Church and portions, at least, of the Eastern Churches, endeavoring to found a Uniate Church, to be approved by the Holy See, perhaps with a vernacular liturgy, and with Clergy bound neither to celibacy nor to marriage, should the Holy See permit.

You understood me rightly when you quoted me as saying that the Church of England remains as "a religious body associated with the national life, but with no just claim to a regular or orthodox position."

Your Grace understands that if the Bishop of London "submitted" to me for re-ordination, I should be prepared "to grant him some official recognition."!

At first sighting nothing could appear more utterly ridiculous.

The smallest, poorest, and most bitterly persecuted fragment of the Catholic Church, extending "official recognition" to the Lord Bishop of London, or to any part or member of the wealthy and still powerful Established religion, would indeed be too absurd for serious notice!

But, in this case, as in many others, things are not precisely what they seem to be.

What are the facts?

The Orders and Sacraments of the Established Church are not officially recognized as valid by any part of the Church Catholic. Indeed, His Holiness Pope Leo XIII condemned them as "absolutely null and utterly void." I do not propose in this letter to enter into the vexed question of the validity of Anglican Orders, but I ask your Grace to consider what would be the consequences of the Bishop of London's conditional baptism, confirmation, ordination and consecration to the Episcopate, at my hands.

It would be this:--Instead of being regarded, of course only in his official capacity, with shyness and doubt, and, in extreme cases, even with contempt, his Lordship's episcopal orders would be "negotiable" in every part of Christendom. It is not a question of my official recognition—which is, comparatively, of little or no importance—but of official recognition by the Catholic Church throughout the world. Moreover, it is more than probable that things would not rest here. The Established Church would soon be able to free herself from her present isolated position. She could so constitute herself,--retaining a married clergy and vernacular liturgy,--that the Holy Father could be approached as to her recognition and constitution as a Uniate Church.

If this were done, and the Establishment were purged from the heresies which at present abound within her, there is, I think, little doubt that the Holy Father would extend to her his paternal care and recognition, as has been done in the case of all the Eastern Uniate Churches. This was my object in suggesting the advisability of re-ordination and consecration, to the Lord Bishop of London, and it is a matter more worthy of Your Grace's serious consideration than your ridicule.*

---

* The Bishop of London was "ordained" priest by Dr. Maclagan when he was Bishop of Lichfield. There is no evidence that Archbishop Maclagan was ever baptised!

"Roman Priest."

For the sake of greater convenience I shall now deal with the insinuations and charges which belong to the earlier part of Your Grace's biographical sketch of me:--

I am quoted as stating that the Established Church was "the church of my Baptism and boyhood."

The circumstances are these:--

I received Baptism shortly after my birth at Montpellier, Hérault, at the hands of a French Abbé. Owing to family differences—which are of no interest to anyone—I was sent to an Anglican Clergyman, and was re-baptised by him, when I was two years of age.

When a boy, at Cheltenham College, I hardly understood the difference between the services at St. Gregory's Catholic Church and those at St. Mary's High Anglican Chuch at Prestbury, and I at times attended both without distinction.

In due course I became aware of my vocation to the Priesthood, and my mother being an Anglican, wished me to enter the Anglican Ministry. My theological studies were accordingly directed to this end. However, the unreality of Anglicanism began to dawn upon me in very early manhood, and I decided in favour of the Roman Catholic Church. I therefore entered a Roman Catholic Seminary.

Having completed the course of studied, and passed the prescribed examination, I was ordained Priest on June 24th, 1877, by the Most Reverend Charles Eyre, Lord Archbishop of Anazarba, i.p.i, afterwards of Glasgow,* who afterwards conferred on me, after the usual examination, a Doctorate in Divinity, which Doctorate was ratified by Pope Pius IX. There is no reference to this matter in your article, but I mention it because even this trivial matter has been made a speculation by some of my critics.

I must say here that in order to prevent difficulties arising at any future date as to my Baptism, the Catholic Authorities thought it advisable that I should receive conditional Baptism before Tonsure, and this precaution was carried out. I might be regarded, by those ignorant of the nature of the Sacrament of Baptism, as a somewhat over-baptised person, but this is at least better than a doubtful Baptism, to say nothing of no Baptism at all!

I continued to exercise my priesthood in the Roman Catholic Church until June, 1889, when, of my own free will, I retired from my benefice—St. Mary's, Bath—to which I had been appointed, in May 1887, by the Hon. and Right Rev. William Clifford, Lord Bishop of Clifton.

The following are the circumstances under which I retired from my charge, and from the exercise of my priesthood in the Roman Catholic Church.

At the time of my appointment to St. Mary's, Bath, I understood that my predecessor, Canon Loughnan, had been obliged to retire for "reasons of health." However, I was not long to remain in ignorance of the true reasons which led to his departure from Bath. I do not, even now, care to think

---

* This was before Pope Leo XIII had restored the Hierarchy to Scotland, when Archbishop Eyre was Vicar Apostolic of the Western District.

of the shock and disgust I experienced as that unhappy man's successor. His subsequent history is a very sad one. Suffice it to say that my position at Bath was unbearable on account of the scandal that he had given. His vices are still well remembered in that City.

At this time, I met an ex-Dominican, an extremely clever man, whose experiences, like my own, had been unpleasant and unfortunate. As a result of conversations with him I resolved to retire, and consequently sent my resignation to the Bishop of Clifton. My disgust and disappointment fully explain the few unguarded things I may have written, at one time and another, with reference to the Roman Catholic Church.

"Count Povoleri."

After my retirement, in 1889, my father asked me to adopt the name Povoleri, and I assumed the name by deed-poll. The title of "Count Povoleri di Nogarole, Vicenza and Verona," was inherited by my father from his mother, the Countess Elisa Francesca Povoleri, eldest daughter and heiress of the Marchese Domenico Povoleri.

I assumed this name and the title of "Count," to which I have every right, because my father wished me to do so, and for no other reason. The matter was legally and openly carried out by my solicitor, and publically advertised. I am not aware that any stigma attaches to Your Grace on account of your grandfather's change of name to Randall to "Davidson."*

On the death of my father, third Earl of Landaff, May 29th, 1894, I resumed my family patronymic, on the advice of Sir Albert Woods, Garter-King-of-Arms. This unimportant matter is recorded in Debrett's "Peerage," etc. The Royal College of Heralds does not recognize a change of name by deed-poll.

"De Jure Earl of Landaff."

Your Grace says that I described myself "as *de jure* Earl of Landaff." The suggestion herein contained would appear to be that my right to do so was open to question.

Though neither merit nor fault of mine I happen to have inherited this title on the death of my father, the third Earl of Landaff, in 1894.

It is not possible for me to devote the considerable sum of money needed to prove, before the Committee of Privileges, my right to vote at the elections of the Irish Representative Peers, nor is it worth my while to do so, at present, since the Landaff peerage is now "bare," all its real estate having been alienated too long ago to be recoverable. I maintain my right to this title, and that it is perfectly legitimate, and according to precedent, for me to make use of it,

---

* Your Grace's grandfather was the Rev. Thomas Randall, Presbyterian Minister of Tolbooth, Edinburgh. On inheriting the Muirhouse estate, Mr. Randall changed his name to "Davidson," otherwise your Grace would now possess "Randall" and not "Davidson" as your surname.

whenever I may choose to do so. It is not a disputed title. There is no rival claimant and there is ample precedent in the Irish Peerage for its use without proof of the right to vote (See Debrett's and Dod's "Peerages," "Who's Who," etc., etc.)

Of what possible use or interest Your Grace's recital of my unimportant private family affairs can be, either to the American Church, or to anyone outside my own domestic circle, I must leave your Grace to explain. All these matters are so many mare's nests!

"Anglican Curate."

I was never an "Anglican Curate"!

In the latter part of 1891, the late Mr. Gladstone and his relation, Margaret Lady Sandhurst, unitedly persuaded me to "make a trial" of the Anglican Ministry, and the late Bishop Temple (then of London, and later on Archbishop of Canterbury), called upon me on several occasions, and was kind enough to state that he thought I might render some service to souls, provided I could satisfy myself that, as an Anglican Clergyman, I should be doing God's Will. Accordingly, I agreed to accept an invitation to go, for a few weeks,--tentatively only—*not as an Anglican,* and *without either license or any ceremony* of "reception into" the Established Church, and without making any sort of kind of assent to the Thirty-nine Articles,--to Holy Trinity Church, Sloan Street, S.W.

The Rector of this Parish was the late Canon Robert Eyton. I had not been in his perish long before I was perceived, to my dismay and horror, that Canon

Eyton was a man of extremely lewd life. His vices took a form particularly repulsive and detestable to me. The grossly immoral life of Canon Eyton (who was later on caught, by a layman, *in flagrante delicto* at St. Margaret's, Westminster), coupled with the fact that Dr. Benson (then Archbishop of Canterbury), required "all ex-Roman Catholic priests," of whom a number were then earning a living as Anglican Clergymen, to subscribe to a "Form of Renunciation of Roman errors" (which proved to be one of the most ignorant and heretical documents I ever beheld), proved too much for me, and caused me to relinquish all thoughts of accepting work in the Establishment. It is true that in 1907 I resented the suggestion that I should spend some period in probationary and subordinate work. Having received a through training in every branch of clerical life, and having been a parish priest for some years, it was only natural that I should do so. At the same time I wish to make it clear that the former reasons constituted my chief difficulty in 1892. I therefore retired again into privacy and seclusion, devoting my time chiefly to literature.

Your Grace next proceeds to criticize my attire:--

You are entirely welcome to any pleasure you may obtain by so doing!

Your Grace next treats of my relations with Holland as an

"Old Catholic Bishop."

I then continued to live for the ensuing fifteen years in seclusion, until 1907. Circumstances which I have already dealt with prevented me either from exercising my priesthood in the Roman Catholic Church, or from becoming a clergyman of the Establishment. During 1907 I received many visits from a suspended Roman Catholic priest, and it was in consequence of conversations with him that I became interested in the Old Roman Catholic Church of Holland, with which he was intimately acquainted.

His representations to me were practically a repetition of statements which has been published five years before I met him in the "Fortnightly Review," for September, 1902, by the Rev. Arthur Galton, then, and still, vicar of an Anglican parish, but formerly a Roman Catholic priest. The same statements, somewhat exaggerated, appeared also in the "Life of Father Ignatius of Llanthony," by the Baroness de Bertouch.* "A great movement" was said to be imminent, and several hundreds of Roman Catholic Clergy were alleged to be interested in it. These statements, in both publications, turned out to be inaccurate, but I was led, at the time, to believe them, and, in consequence of them, to turn my thoughts to an Old Roman Catholic Movement for England.

Up to this time the Old Roman Catholic Church of Holland had very jealously guarded the validity of her Orders, and had taken no liberties with the Catholic Faith, which she had preserved absolutely intact. Indeed, a competent Roman Catholic Authority, after examining her books o

* Methuen & Co.

devotion, was able to say that they contained no heresy nor anything to which Roman Catholics could take exception.† Here was the very thing for which I had been looking, and I thought, quite reasonably, that, as was alleged, there might be a large number of others, who, like myself, being unable to exercise their ministry either as Roman Catholics or as Members of the Establishment, would welcome an Old Roman Catholic Mission in England.

Later on, arrangements were made by the priest to whom I have alluded, in conjunction with Dr. Herzog, "Christian Catholic" Bishop at Berne, for providing the Old Roman Catholic Movement in this country with a Bishop. During this time I continued to live in seclusion, and saw nothing of those who were said to be interested in the Movement, other than the suspended priest mentioned above. I had nothing whatever to do with any of the arrangements or negotiations for providing the Movement with a Bishop, and was not a little surprised when, shortly afterwards, I was informed that I had myself received the honour of election as "the first Bishop for the work." I had no wish to be a bishop, my election gratified no private ambition,--quite the contrary. I reluctantly, under pressure, submitted to the election. My Consecration was arranged to take place on April 8th, 1908. When I arrived at Utrecht, I was informed by Archbishop Gul that the consecration could not take place on that date, because I was a married man! It has been said that the Old Roman Catholic Bishops had "unexpectedly become aware" that I was a married man. This suggests concealment. I cannot say

---

† See A Catholic Dictionary, article "Dutch Jansenists."

whether my marriage had been deliberately concealed or not. It is quite possible that those who had charge of the arrangements considered it unnecessary to mention an important but domestic detail of this kind, or it may have been an oversight. In any case, as I had nothing to do with the arrangements, no blame can be attached to me. My marriage took place as far back as my retirement, in February, 1892. There was nothing either secret or clandestine about the proceeding, and the suspended priest, who visited me, was perfectly well aware that I was a married man. It was an incident recorded year by year in Debrett, etc. This I explained to the Archbishop of Utrecht. The Dutch Clergy observed clerical celibacy, and had not, then, consecrated a married priest. However, Dr. Cech, the Bishop-elect of the Austrian Old Catholics, was a married priest, and the German Old Catholic Bishop at Bonn—Dr. Moog—is also married.

As I had been elected, the Archbishop of Utrecht submitted the matter to the Dutch Clergy, and they decided in favour of my consecration, which accordingly took place at Utrecht on April 28th, 1908, Archbishop Gul being the Consecrator, the Bishops of Haarlem, Deventer, and Bonn acting as the Assistant-Bishops. I have already dealt with Dr. Herzog's absurd recent invention that my consecration was "rendered null and void by fraud"!

Your Grace goes on to say that:--"The subsequent story does not appear to be of sufficient importance to make it necessary to narrate its particulars. It is not evident that any public purpose would be served by an endeavor to explain the successive changes of designation—and the breach which very speedily took place between Bishop Mathew and the Old Catholic Bishops, and then between Bishop Mathew and, it would seem, most of those who have claimed to have received Presbyteral or Episcopal Orders at his hands."

I will take these statements *seriatim:--*

"Changes of Designation."

These are so unimportant that they hardly deserve passing notice. No two of them are contradictory, nor do any of them signify any "change" either of Faith or of principles. Some of these designations happen to have been placed not by me, but by the Baroness Natalie d'Uxkull, upon documents composed and printed by her, in which the Movement was described and to which my name was appended. The title "Western Orthodox Church" was intended and applied to a*ll* the Old Catholics by the late General Alexander Kiréeff, whose sister, Madame Olga Novikoff, is a particular friend of our Movement. The French periodical edited by my friend Mgr. de Lignières before the War, contained his own, and not my, description of myself. As I did not see or hear of it, until it had been printed or circulated, I cannot see or hear of it, until it had been printed and circulated, I can hardly be held responsible for its appearance. I did not, then, change "*from Old Catholic Bishop to French Archbishop*" !!

There is, or was before the War, and Old Roman Catholic Mission in France, which looked to me as its provisional head. I never relinquished my position as head of the French Movement. It is not easy to speak of the French Mission at the present time, as the Clergy took their places in the French Army when war was declared, and some of them have been killed.

In the Church over which you preside there are many who will not admit its official title. There are many more who are far from being proud of it.

Again, your church is known by many and conflicting names, each representing one or other of the many "Schools of Thought" for which that "comprehensive" body is so notorious. Had you taken the trouble to scan the columns containing advertisements for Curates and Curacies in any Anglican newspaper, I think you would have thought twice before mentioning varieties of designation! Now I come to *"the breach which speedily took place between Bishop Mathew and the Old Catholic Bishops."*

The breach did not take place for two years and eight months after my Consecration. Though this is not a long time, it can hardly be said with truth that the breach took place "speedily."

You say that "It is not evident that any public purpose would be served by an endeavor to explain" these things. Your Grace has not made the slightest attempt to "explain" anything of your article, nor had you any intention of explaining. You merely wished to represent certain of my actions in an unfair and unfavourable light, in order to create and foster prejudice against me. It is strange that you should consider my private family affairs of more importance than the subsequent history of my public work, and it would be stranger still if, after giving the above list, and treating it as you have chosen to do, you should be willing to commence giving explanations of the matter now under consideration. It is not a question of "serving any public purpose," my Lord, but rather your Grace's own ends!

Consequently you are careful to suppress the *causes* which led to our separation from the See of Utrecht, and the *date* at which it took place.

For the same reason, no mention is made of the fact that the Movement was received into union with the Eastern Orthodox Church in August, 1911, and that it remains so united.

Your Grace was well aware that these facts would tell in our favour. Again, it is hardly to be expected that you would run the risk of involving yourself in any dispute with the Old Catholic Bishops, or with the Catholic party in your own church, by stating that I severed the English Movement from the See of Utrecht, because the Dutch Old Roman Catholic Bishops had begun to tamper with Catholic teaching and practice. In order to curry favour with German opinion, the standard of Faith had been considerably lowered in Holland, and an attempt had been made to minimize the differences between the Catholic Faith, Calvinism, and Lutheranism. It is much easier, and very much more convenient to suggest that the Old Catholic Bishops took the initiative and cut me off in disgust. However, the suggestion does not happen to be true.

Once again let me draw attention to the facts of the case. Many Anglicans wished to make use of the ministrations of my clergy, and to receive the Sacraments at their hands. The "Society of St.

Willibrord" was founded by the Rev. George Edward Barber, Senior Curate at St. James's Church, Hampstead Road, N.W., to promote friendly relations between the Establishment and ourselves. I found it necessary to withdraw from the "Society of St. Willibrord."

I shall have occasion to refer to this Society and to its Founder, Mr. Barber, a little later on. Proposals for intercommunion with the Established Church rendered it necessary that the question of the validity of Anglican Orders, together with the advisability, or otherwise, of such intercommunion, would receive careful thought and attention. My decision that "Anglican Orders were at best extremely doubtful" was published on June 7th, 1910. (Both sides of the case are exhaustively dealt with in my little book, "Are Anglican Orders Valid?" It contains an attempt at a defense of Anglican Orders by the Ch*urch Times* and by Mr. Hakluyt Egerton. Many authorities are cited, and the vital question of the validity of Baptism received by many Anglican Prelates—Your Grace amongst them—is dealt with at length. The book can still be obtained, and may be interesting to all who are in any way affected by these all-important matters.) It would seem that the Dutch Bishops, under Mr. Barber's influence, were inclined to give Anglican Orders the benefit of the doubt, and, on August 5th, 1910, a little over four months before I declared the independence of the English Movement, the following letter appeared in the *Guardian*, the Bishop van Thiel having written it at Mr. Barber's request:--

"SIR,

"Having seen in your issue of July, 29th, Mr. Barber's letter on the Society of St. Willibrord, I wish to say that Mr. Barber is quite right in stating in his letter of last week that Bishop Mathew is in no sense a representative of the Church of Holland in England. Bishop Mathew is simply one of the Old Catholic Bishops, and, as such, he is in relation with the Old Catholics of Holland, and also, of course, with the Old Catholic Churches of Germany, Switzerland, and Austria, the Polish Catholic Church of America, and the Catholic Church of the Mariavites in Poland.

"In consequence of that, I wish to state that the Old Catholics in Holland and elsewhere could not be considered in any way responsible for Bishop Mathew's eventual particular attitude or opinions, because he only represents his own clergy and himself in England.

+ J. J. VAN THIEL,
"Bishop of Haarlem."

I have never claimed to "represent the Church of Holland" or any other Catholic Churches. It was I who had to deal with the question of Anglican Intercommunion, and, consequently, to decide whether or not we could recognize Anglican Orders.

Nothing could be more absurd than to expect the Dutch Church to "accept responsibility" in a matter in which they came so little into contact, and it is more than probable that, but for Mr. Barber's meddlesomeness, the Dutch Bishops would never have troubled themselves with the question at all.

However, nothing happens by chance, and this letter is now of value in that it proves that the Dutch Bishops *already regarded our English Movement as autonomous*, as are all other sections or "branches" of the Old Catholic Church,--and it is yet another proof—if indeed further proof were required—of the untruthfulness of Dr. Herzog's latest theory, which is being put forward in America just now, to the effect that the misrepresentations made to the Dutch Bishops as to our numbers, etc., rendered my Consecration "null and void"! It does most clearly prove that I was in full communion with the Dutch Old Catholics, until I withdrew the English Movement from communion with them in December, 1910. I have already briefly cited the reasons for my separation, but in order that the matter may be better understood, I append the Pastoral Letter containing our Declaration of Independence and Autonomy:--

"A PASTORAL LETTER ISSUED ON 29TH DECEMBER, 1910.

"DECLARATION OF AUTONOMY AND INDEPENDENCE.

"We, the undersigned Bishop, on behalf of our clergy and Laity of the Catholic Church of England, hereby proclaim and declare the autonomy and independence of our portion of the One Holy Catholic and Apostolic Church.

"We are in no way whatever subject to or dependent on any foreign See, nor do we recognize the right of nay members of the religious bodies known as "Old Catholics" on the Continent, to require submission from us to their authority or jurisdiction, or to the decrees, decisions, rules, or enactments of any of their Conventions, Synods, Congresses, or other assemblies, in which we have neither taken part nor expressed our agreement.

"The venerable Church of the Netherlands, which is a British and Irish Foundation, due to the apostolic labours of St. Willbrord and St. Boniface, and consolidated by the efforts of other Saints an Monks of the ancient Churches of England and Ireland, remained staunch and true to its primitive Catholic belief, traditions and customs for more than twelve centuries.

"With inexpressible joy, therefore, did we, in the year 1907, receive the sacred Episcopate, to be restored to our country through the instrumentality of His Grace the Most Reverend Lord Archbishop of Utrecht, Mgr. Gul, who presides over the small remnant of the ancient English Church still surviving in the Netherlands. Whilst retaining our profound respect for and gratitude to this estimable Prelate, we cannot but express the deep regret we feel that our hopes should have been disappointed in the way we now describe:

"We had supposed and believed that the Faith, once for all delivered to the Saints, and set forth in the decrees of the Councils accepted as Œcumenical no less in the West than in the East, would have continued unimpaired, whether by augmentation or by diminution, in the venerable Church of the Dutch Nation.

"We anticipated that the admirable fidelity with which the Bishops and Clergy of that Church had adhered to the Faith and handed it down, untarnished by heresy, notwithstanding grievous persecution and opposition during so many centuries, would never have wavered.

"Unfortunately, however, we discover, with dismay, pain and regret, that the standards of Orthodoxy, laid down of old by the Fathers and the Councils of the East and West alike, having been departed from in various particulars by certain sections of Old Catholicism, these departures, indeed of being checked and repressed, are, at least tacitly, tolerated and acquiesced in without protest, by the Hierarchy of the Church of the Netherlands.

"In order to avoid misapprehension, we here specify nine of the points of difference between the Continental Old Catholics and ourselves:--

"(1). Although the Synod of Jerusalem, under Dositheus in 1672, was not an Œcumenical Council, its decrees are accepted by the Holy Orthodox Church of the Orient as accurately expressing its belief, and are in harmony with the decrees of the Council of Trent on the dogmas of which they treat. We are in agreement with the Holy Orthodox Church, regarding this Synod, and we therefore accept and endorse the Decrees of the aforesaid Synod of Jerusalem. Hence, we hold and declare that there are Seven Holy Mysteries or Sacraments, all of them instituted by our Divine Lord and Saviour Jesus Christ, therefore all of them necessary for the salvation of mankind, though all are not necessarily to be received by ever individual, *e.g.* Holy Orders and Matrimony.

"Certain sections, if not all, of the Old Catholic bodies, reject this belief, and refuse assent to the decrees of the Holy Synod of Jerusalem.

"(2). Moreover, some of them have abolished the Sacrament of Penance by condemning and doing away with auricular confession; others actively discourage this salutary practice; others, again, whilst tolerating its use, declare the Sacrament of Penance to be merely optional, therefore unnecessary, and of no obligation, even for those who have fallen into mortal sin after Baptism.

"(3). In accordance with the belief and practice of the Universal Church, we adhere to the doctrine of the Communion of Saints by invoking and venerating the Blessed Virgin Mary, and those who have received the crown of glory in heaven, as well as the Holy Angels of God.

"The Holy Catholics in the Netherlands have not yet all together abandoned this pious and helpful custom, but, in some other countries, invocation of the Saints has been totally abolished by the Old Catholics. Even the Angelic Salutation, or *Ave Maria*, familiar to the lips of every Christian, is no longer recited by them, and from the various newly-devised vernacular liturgies, the name of the Saints have been omitted.

"(4). Although it may be permissible, and indeed, very disable, in some countries, and under certain circumstances to render the Liturgy into vernacular languages, we consider it to be neither expedient nor tolerable that individuals should compose new liturgies, according to their own particular views, or make alterations, omissions and changes in venerable rites to suit their peculiar fancies, prejudices or idiosyncrasies. We lament the mutilations of this kind which have occurred among the Old Catholics in several countries, and regret that no two of the new liturgies composed and published by them are alike, either in form or in ceremony. In all of them the ancient rubrics have been set aside, and the ceremonies and symbolism with which the sacred Mysteries of the Altar have been reverently environed for many centuries, have, either wholly or in part, been ruthlessly swept away. The Rite of Benediction of the Blessed Sacrament has also been almost universally abolished among the Old Catholics.

"(5). Since the time of the Venerable Bede, 'Old Rome,' 'the Imperial City,' has always been regarded as the religious capital of Western Christendom, just as 'New Rome'—Constantinople—became the religious capital of Eastern Christendom.

"We, therefore, treading in the footsteps of our Catholic forefathers, and in accordance with the decrees of the Œcumenical Councils, regard the Bishop of Old Rome as the Primate of Christendom and as Patriarch of the West, and our desire is to exhibit due respect and veneration for the person of His Holiness in that exalted station.

"In accordance with the primitive teaching of the Church of the Netherlands, which prevailed until a very recent date, we consider it a duty on the part of Western Christians to remember His Holiness the Pope as their Patriarch in their prayers and sacrifices. The name of His Holiness should, therefore, retain its position in the Canon of the Mass, where, as we observed at our consecration in Utrecht, it was customary, and remained so until a recent date in the present year (1910), for the celebrant to recite the name of our Patriarch in the usual manner in the Mass and in the Litany of the Saints. The publication of a new vernacular Dutch Liturgy in the present year causes us to regret that the clergy of Holland are now required to omit the name of His Holiness in the Canon of the Mass. Happily, only a small number of other alterations in the text of the Canon have, so far, been introduced. These, however, include the audible recitation of the whole of the secret prayers of the Mass, and the omission of the prayer *Hæc Commixtio,* also the omission of the title 'ever Virgin' whenever it occurs in the Latin Missal.

"Such alterations pave the way for others of an even more serious nature, which may be made in the future, and, as we think, are to be deplored.

"Among other sections of Old Catholicism not only have all public prayers for the Western Patriarch been abandoned, but the historical position and legitimate and generally-recognized prerogatives of His Holiness have been ignored, whilst, by some, a tone of bitterness and vulgar insolence has been introduced in referring to the Roman Pontiff, which is only comparable to that adopted by the most vituperative, ignorant and inveterate of the Protestant sects. This attitude we deeply regret, and entirely dissociate ourselves from it. *Caritas benigna est.*

"(6). Following the example of our Catholic forefathers, we venerate the adorable Sacrifice of the Mass as the supreme act of Christian worship, instituted by Christ Himself.

"Since, during very many centuries, it has been the custom, throughout the Western Church, for the clergy to celebrate daily, we require our clergy to fulfill this sacred duty, exulting in the privilege and benefitting by the graces which thus become theirs.

"We grieve that the Old Catholic clergy, in most countries, have abandoned the daily celebration of Mass, and now limit the offering of the Christian Sacrifice to Sundays and a few of the greater Feasts.

"The corresponding neglect of the Blessed Sacrament, and infrequency of Holy Communion, on the part of the laity are marked.

"(7). In accordance both with Catholic custom and with the decrees of the Œcumenical Councils, we hold that the honour and glory of God are promoted and increased by the devout and religious use of holy pictures, statues, symbols, relics, and the like, as aids to devotion, and that, in relation to those they represent, they are to be held in veneration. The Old Catholics have, generally speaking, preferred to dispense with such helps to piety.

"(8). We consider that the Holy Sacraments should be administered only to those who are members of the Holy Catholic Church, not only by Baptism, but by the profession of the Catholic Faith in its integrity, by repudiation of all heresies, by rejection of any bond of union, and refusal of actual communion, with all persons and sects professing unorthodox beliefs, whether as individuals, or by formularies to which they are committed. Unhappily, we find persons who are not Catholics, of whose baptism and orthodoxy there is no certainty, and who are members of denominations professing heretical tenets, are now admitted, without even conditional baptism or confession or profession of faith, to receive Holy Communion in all the Old Catholic places of worship on the Continent. Although Communion under one species is still regarded as sufficient, non-Catholic desiring Communion under both species are thus communicated out of deference to their tenets.

"Moreover, clergymen of the Anglican Communion, whose Orders are open to the gravest doubt, have been permitted to celebrate the 'Service for the Administration of Holy Communion' from the Anglican book of devotion, entitled 'The Book of Common Prayer,' at Old Catholic altars, thus causing both Catholics and Protestants to suppose that Anglican Orders are accepted as valid by the Old Catholics in general.

"(9). The Old Catholics have ceased to observe the prescribed days of fasting and abstinence, and no longer observe the custom of receiving Holy Communion fasting.

"For these and other reasons, which it is unnecessary to detail, we, the undersigned Bishop, desire, by these presents, to declare our autonomy and our independence of all foreign interference in our doctrine, discipline, and policy. *In necessariis unitas, in dubiis libertas, in omnibus caritas.*

"Given under our hand and sealed with our deal this 29th day of December, the Feast of St. Thomas of Canterbury, in the year of our Lord one thousand nine hundred and ten.

+ "ARNOLD H. MATHEW."

This is the whole story of the "Breach," except that at a Meeting, held in the Church House, London, three years later, *i.e.*, in November, 1913, a question, which had been previously arranged at Mr. Barber's instigation, was put to Dr. Prins, the new Bishop of Haarlem, regarding my "position." Bishop Prins did not himself reply, but directed Father Gol, of Gouda, to read a prepared typewritten answer, to the effect that the Dutch Bishops, at the last Old Catholic Congress held in September, 1913, decided "not to recognize me or any of my acts." No reasons were given, and I have never received any official communications from the Dutch Bishops. This farcical denunciation actually took place three years after I had already withdrawn from communion with the foreign Old Catholic bodies.

Concerning **"The breach between Bishop Mathew and most of those who for a time claimed to have received Presbyteral or Episcopal Orders at his hands."**

Some of those whom I have ordained, are no longer connected with our Movement. Of these, some have felt it their duty to submit to the Holy See, some others, through poverty, have had to undertake secular work for a time, and these are still my excellent friends. As we are most careful to do nothing in the nature of tolerating heresy or condoning vice, a few have been suspended. Two of the last came to me from the Anglican Church. It has been publicly stated that one of these, when an

Anglican Clergyman, had lived a most scandalous life. The other ministered in that communion for twenty years, without ever having received ordination of any sort or kind!

Had the Anglican Bishops who were responsible for these individuals acted with more justice and wisdom, and less sentiment, much trouble would have been saved, and certainly one of them would have been unable to excite the friendly help and pity of the adherents of our Movement by posing as a martyr. So far as I know, only three of those ordained by me have sought your help or that of the Bishop of London, and I cannot imagine what they mean if they state that "they had acted under a misapprehension," nor can it be said *with truth* by anyone ordained by me. One of these men—a German—holds, or held, the Bishop of London's license to officiate in Anglican Churches in German, French and Latin for the "benefit" of foreign "Old Catholics"! It is difficult to understand why this person should have been so licensed, unless the object was to injure and discredit my work.

There can be little object in discussing my action, in 1913, for libel against the *Times* Publishing Company. It is generally agreed, I believe, in legal circles, that I was shamefully handled. At any rate, it is true that both Your Grace and the Roman Catholic Authorities produced irrelevant private and confidential letters from me—some of them thirteen years old,--and caused them to be read in open court. The acts of Parliament of Elizabeth, 1559, and Victoria, 1846, were clearly on my side. Again, very great assistance and information were given by the unscrupulous curate Barber, which enabled skilful and vituperative counsel to weave a narrative, utterly misapprehending the points at issue, but so representing the action as to prejudice and confuse a middle-class jury of Protestants, who, however unbiased, were utterly incapable of understanding such a case. Had the *Times* Company not succeeded in blocking and preventing my appeal, I am perfectly confident that the verdict over which you and Mr. Barber exulted, would have been absolutely set aside. I will take this opportunity of pointing out that certain unfriendly individuals in America have confounded this case with another, in an attempt to besmirch my reputation. I therefore add that I was never "sued by a Miss Mathew" nor has "the Crown or the House of Lords" ever "denied" my "right to the peerage of Landaff."

Conclusion

I believe that I have now answered all the ingenious insinuations contained in your letter and memorandum. Other charges, ranging from dishonour to absurdity and even lunacy have, I believe, been covertly (but never openly) made against me. Moreover, it is noteworthy that my friends have heard no hint of the former kind since Mr. Barber's death. I can only say that such charges which may have been made are utterly groundless and absolutely without foundation.

I have said that I should again refer to Mr. Barber and the Society of St. Willibrord, which he did so much to establish, in order to bring about friendly relations and intercommunion between the Established Church and the Old Catholics. I do so in order to explain why Mr. barber should have constituted himself the most bitter of our enemies, and have spared himself no effort which might be calculated to harm my reputation or damage my work.

The reason is very simple. In 1910 I found it necessary to decline the late Mr. Barber's further acquaintance, owing to the discovery of the appalling immorality and vileness of his private life. He resented my action, and the more so because he was unable to give me any reasonable or even plausible explanation or excuse for the termination of our acquaintance. From this time forward hatred, spite and malice inspired and prompted him to every effort which might be calculated to injure me and wreck my work.

On two occasions this man had appeared before the Bishop of London to answer charges of an unmentionable kind. I ought, perhaps, to support what I have said. Evidence, including a report of the trial of Ross v. Lord Alfred Douglas (which, I believe, was kept out of the newspapers at the request of the Bishop of London), is before me as I write.* At first I thought of publishing it in full, but having said all that is absolutely necessary in my own defense, the matter shall rest here, unless further persecution should render it necessary for me to be more explicit. Why such a man was allowed to continue his ministry, or why he should have the power to

* See Press reports of November, 1914, and January, 1915, Rex v. Ross.

influence Your Grace, the Bishop of London, and many others, against my work and myself, must remain to us an inexplicable mystery. That the Bishops of London and Willesden should have thought it necessary to give his remains a solemn "pontifical" burial, and that the *Guardian* and the *Church Times* should have panegyrized him after his decease, must for years to come cause infinite astonishment to all who regard the corruption of the young as the most atrocious crime of which any man can be guilty. To think of such iniquities is indeed extremely horrible and distressing, but to have to cite them, even in defense of one's work and character (and I have had the Movement more in mind than myself) is painful beyond description. My silence, in the past five years, testifies to my extreme unwillingness to bring these matters before the public. I regret that my enemies have not scrupled to misrepresent and make adverse use of my silence, and so, at last, they have forced me to write what I would only too gladly have put out of my mind for ever.

With these hostile persons, and with those who have constantly persecuted me and my associated, the responsibility for any pain that may be caused to the friends of those whom I have had to mention, must rest.

Our body is small and extremely poor. So poor, indeed, that its indigence defies description. My clergy receive no remuneration or emoluments whatsoever, and work without hope, and, it would seem, without prospect of any early reward for their labours. There is not a man at present with me who has not jeopardized his all, and some of my clergy have made sacrifices which they would not allow me to mention, in order to carry on the work which we honestly believe Almighty God has committed to us. As yet we see little result beyond failure and disappointment. The greatness of our work in the interests of Re-union is the measure of our trial, and, when we have proved ourselves more worthy, we may yet be blessed to the extent of seeing that our toil has not been wholly in vain. The Movement will go on in spite of all difficulties, and notwithstanding the persecution and scorn of our enemies, however severe it may be. As to Your Grace, I am truly sorry that you have so far forgotten the dignity of your exalted position as to descend to the unfair methods of argument which you have adopted in order to hurt a defenseless old Bishop, and to try to ruin his work. I bear Your Grace no malice, and forgive you any personal damage your letter and memorandum may have done me. I pray that Almighty God may pardon all that you, and those associated with you, have done to obstruct and mar the work which He has given us to do.

I have the honour to be,
My Lord Archbishop,
Your Grace's most obedient servant,
+ Arnold H. Mathew,
Old Roman Catholic Archbishop.

KINGSDOWN,
NR. WALMER,
Feast of All Saints, 1915.

www.ingramcontent.com/pod-product-compliance
Ingram Content Group UK Ltd.
Pitfield, Milton Keynes, MK11 3LW, UK
UKHW041834200726
13854UKWH00003BA/1140